The Adventures of Bonnie the Little White Horse

Written by
Aaron Barnes

Illustrated by
Jane Fryer

© Aaron Barnes 2024
All Rights Reserved

Once upon a time there was a little white horse called Bonnie who just loved to go for very exciting long walks with her walking hat and her little umbrella.

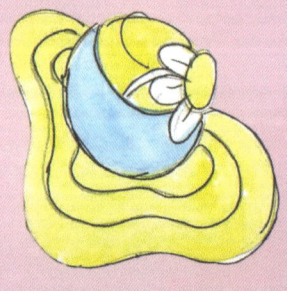

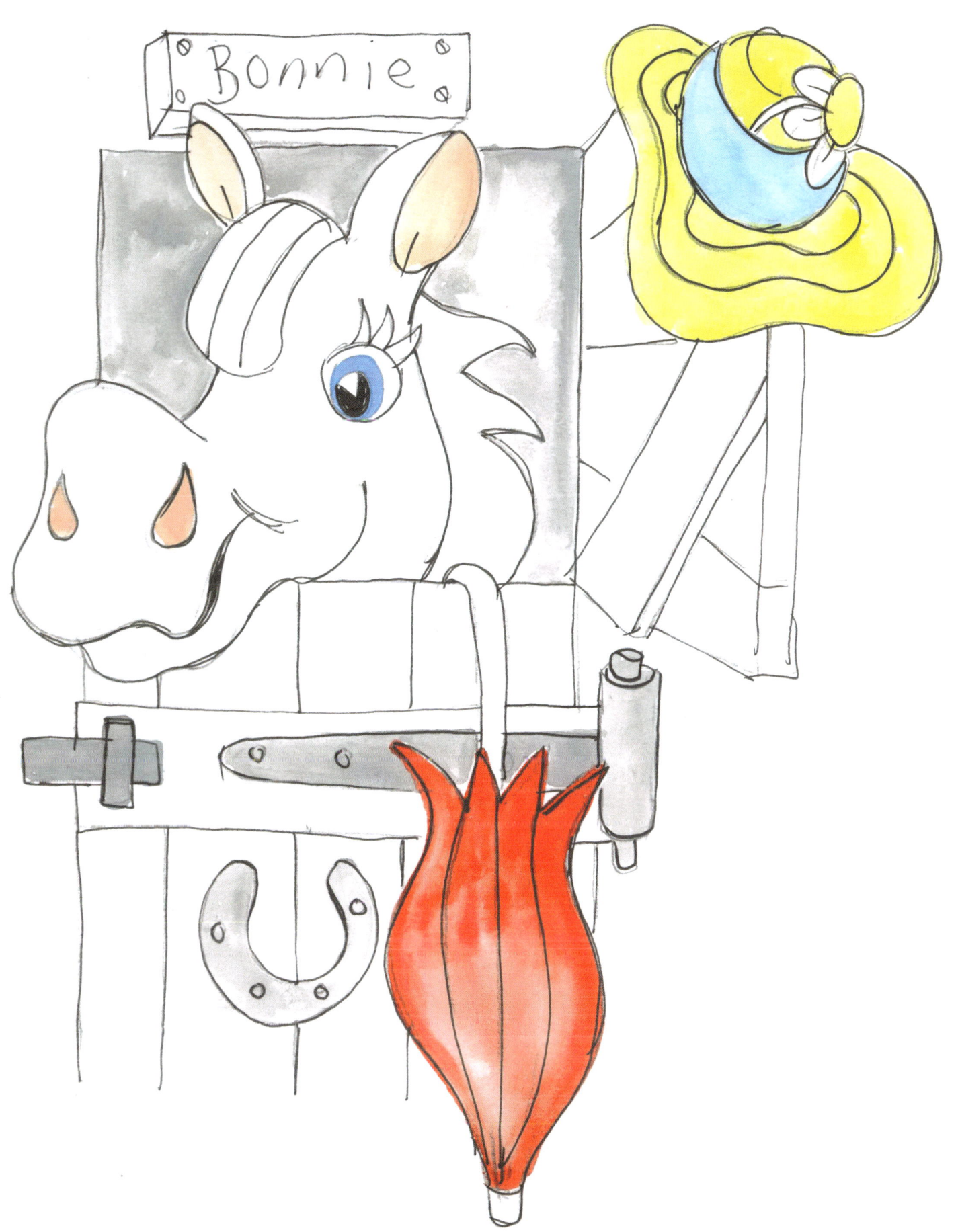

One day Bonnie the little white horse decided she would go for a very exciting long walk along the canal path where there would be lots of wildlife, so she gathered her walking hat and her little umbrella in case it rained and off she trotted, clip clop, clip clop.

Just minutes along the canal path Bonnie the little white horse could see a very fast swan swimming towards her so she quickly put up her little umbrella and tried to hide behind it.

"Hello" said the swan, "I can see you hiding behind your little umbrella misses horse, I am Suzie, Suzie the swan, and what is your name?"

"Oh, well hello Suzie the swan, I am Bonnie the little white horse and I just love to go for walks, would you like to join me on a very exciting long walk along the canal path?"

"Well thank you." replied Suzie the swan "I would really enjoy a nice long walk with you Bonnie the little white horse, but where are we going?"

So Suzie the swan jumped up out of the canal onto the path and followed Bonnie the little white horse on a very exciting long walk along the canal path.

Moments later Bonnie the little white horse and Suzie the beautiful swan heard a rustle coming from the bushes just ahead of them, so up popped the little umbrella and Bonnie the horse and Suzie the swan tried to hide behind it.

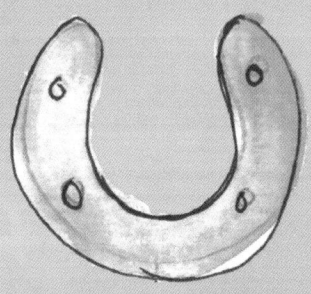

But in a flash out jumped a little brown rat and said "Hello little white horse and beautiful swan trying to hide behind that little umbrella, I can see you, I am Reggie, Reggie the rat and who may you two be?"

"Oh hello." Reggie the rat replied, the little white horse and beautiful swan swiftly followed by "I am Bonnie the little white horse and I am Suzie the beautiful swan and we're going for a very exciting long walk, would you like to join us Reggie rat?"

"Oh, well how exciting." said Reggie the rat, "that would just be fantastic, but I am so small I would never keep up with you both, would you mind if I ride on your back Bonnie the little white horse?"

"Of course," replied Bonnie "I would not mind at all." So Reggie the rat climbed upon Bonnie the horse and off they set along the canal path on a very exciting long walk.

Moments later Bonnie the little white horse, Suzie the beautiful swan, oh and Reggie the little brown rat could see the water in the canal rippling ahead of them, so up popped the little umbrella and Bonnie the horse, Suzie the swan and of course Reggie the rat tried their very best to hide behind it. But swimming across the surface of the water was a very long and green snake.

"Hello little white horse and beautiful swan, oh and fluffy little brown rat trying to hide behind that little umbrella, I am Simon, Simon the snake, who may you three be?"

"Oh, hello," Simon the snake replied. The little white horse, the beautiful swan, and, of course, the fluffy little brown rat swiftly followed.
"I am Bonnie the little white horse."
"And I am Suzie the beautiful swan."
"I am Reggie the fluffy brown rat, and we're going for a very long and exciting walk. Would you like to join us?"

"Indeed, I would love to!" replied Simon the snake, "I would like that very much, but I cannot help the terrifying hissing noise I seem to make, please don't be frightened of me following you on your very exciting long walk."

"It's ok," replied Bonnie the horse, "we don't mind." So Simon the snake followed along as they set off along the canal path on their very exciting long walk.

They were all having such fun on their very exciting long walk when all of a sudden there were loud noises of thunder, crashes of lightening and it began to rain.

"Don't worry everyone," said Bonnie the little white horse, "I have bought my special little walking umbrella to keep us dry, we can all take shelter underneath."

So Bonnie the horse popped up her little umbrella once again whilst Simon the very long and green snake, Reggie the fluffy brown rat and Suzie the beautiful swan all tried their very best to squeeze under the little umbrella to keep dry.

"It's just no good," cried Reggie the rat, "we will never all stay dry under here, I am going to burrow deep into the canal bank to make a new home and stay dry. Goodbye Simon the snake, Suzie the swan and Bonnie the little white horse." said Reggie "It's been lovely meeting you all."

"Goodbye!" they all replied to Reggie the rat as he burrowed deep into the bank of the canal.

"Well I don't mind getting wet," said Simon the snake "After all, I am a hissing watersnake, so I shall leave you both to it." he said to Suzie the swan and Bonnie the little white horse, "It's been so much fun meeting you on your very exciting walk along the canal path, goodbye!" he said.

"Goodbye!" replied Bonnie the horse and Suzie the swan "It's been lots of fun meeting you." And Simon set off back across the canal.

"Well then," Bonnie the little white horse said to Suzie the beautiful swan, "I guess that's the end of our very exciting long walk along the canal path, it must be home time where I can get some rest in my nice, dry, warm stable."

"Goodbye Suzie the swan, it's been lovely meeting you today on my very exciting long walk."

"Goodbye Bonnie the horse," replied Suzie the swan "I've had so much fun." as she hopped back into the canal and swam off happily.

When Bonnie the little white horse arrived home she got herself all cosy in her stable, still wearing her walking hat and holding her little umbrella in her mouth.

She thought to her self what a fantastic day she had meeting Suzie the swan, Reggie the rat and Simon the snake on her very exciting long walk along the canal path and could not wait to do it all over again the next day.

The End.

Printed in Great Britain
by Amazon